Frugal Psychology

How to Develop a Frugal Mindset and Secure Your Financial Security

Preface

Take charge of your money and attain dizzying heights of financial security.

This guide has been written for every person who has never received any sort of training or information on **how to manage their money properly**. It is a guide to show you **the power of living frugally** and how that can quickly pay off in dividends if you stick with it long enough.

With this guide as your launching pad, you'll learn the ABCs and 123s of money as you've never been taught before. You'll discover the secrets of transitioning from working multiple jobs to **developing a life of freedom** and fun through frugal living.

Table of Contents

Introduction

So many people live their lives without knowing exactly how to handle their finances. Ask the average person, and they're resigned to feeling like one day they'll run out, and that's the end of the world for them. They have no idea how to handle their situation. For too many people, the strategy is to bury their heads in the sand and hope that things miraculously work out for the best. Can you relate to this feeling? Do you struggle with a sense of anxiety and impending doom when it comes to your financial future? Are you terrified about how to handle yourself when you're no longer in a position to work?

This book has been written for people who've never had an opportunity to learn about how money works and how they can turn their seemingly meager incomes into vehicles for financial security and freedom. If you're one of these people, you've chosen the perfect guide to learn how to take back your financial power.

It has been written in understandable English so that every concept presented is easy to grasp. It is packed full of practical advice that will lead you to a more empowered financial position than you've ever experienced. Unlike other books on the matter, this one does away with unnecessarily complicated jargon and focuses on the practical stuff that has always worked. It gets right down to the meat of the matter, helping you chart a path from wage slavery to ultimate freedom.

Taking charge of your finances doesn't have to be rocket science, nor should it leave you with a migraine. Thanks to this book, you'll discover that the process is relatively simple, and all you have to do is remain consistent. It is impossible not to see improvement in your finances when you religiously follow all the practical tips offered.

Are you ready to transform the state of your financial life? Are you sick and tired of waking up every day feeling anxious about your future? Are you prepared to walk the path that leads you to the ultimate goal of firing your boss? If you've answered yes to these questions, head to the first chapter and follow everything you learn to the letter. Someday, your future self will thank you for daring to take this path.

Chapter 1

Introduction to Frugal Psychology

If you want to ensure a secure financial future, then you have to learn to be frugal. But what exactly does that mean? You need to become conscious of your spending habits and honestly analyze them to see what you need to cut out and what you should do more of. Unless you're Bezos or Soros, you have a limited amount of resources, so you have to think about what you should do to manage your money better. Many people thumb their noses at the idea of frugality because, in their minds, it implies never getting to live life or enjoy the dollars they've worked hard for. However, that's not what it is about.

You can still be frugal and allow yourself some luxuries within reason. It's simply about looking for every chance to make each penny stretch as far as it can before you have to dip into your pockets to pull out another. This is the path to financial freedom, boring as it may sound, but at the very least, you'll enjoy not feeling anxious every time you think of your pockets or account balance. Being frugal allows you to handle emergencies as well as pursue your dreams and make investments that pay off handsomely when the opportunities present themselves.

The Principles behind Frugality

Paying Attention to Your Needs: It's time to stop caring what's happening with your neighbors when it comes to money. Sure, they may have bought another Ferarri and gone on five vacations in the current year, even if it's not even March yet, but that doesn't mean you need to live the same life they have, not if you can't afford it. Become blind to others' experiences and choices, and instead, make your choices based on your personal goals and what you can afford. If you're used to buying stuff you really don't need with money that's barely there — if not borrowed — and for the sole purpose of impressing people who probably don't care either way about what you do or don't have, you've got to put an end to that now. This principle is about waiting patiently before making purchases to be certain it's something you really need and not simply a want. By following this idea, you'll avoid slipping into "lifestyle creep," where you begin spending more and more when your income goes up. Getting a raise doesn't mean you should spend it all right away.

Thinking Long-Term Rather Than Short-Term: There will be times when it's much better to make a big spend because that's the better option over the long term. In other words, if you know there's something you will likely need in the future, and that item is going to cost far more later than now, then it makes sense to get it now. Then there are times when it's better to spend more because quality items last much longer. If you choose the cheaper stuff, what happens is you'll spend more in the long run, replacing the item over and over. In other words, it's better to buy a couch for $500 if it will last for seven years than to get one for $50 that you'll have to keep replacing every six months. When you cannot get higher-quality items because you can't afford them, and it's not a legitimate need, then it's best to forget about it. Also, beware: Something being expensive doesn't always mean it's of great quality.

Caring about the Price of Things: Are you the sort of person who chucks things into their cart without looking at the prices? Well, it's time to start checking because you'd be surprised how much you could save by choosing alternate brands that are just as good (and sometimes better) than the pricey ones you've been using. So, rather than look at the brand names first, look at the prices first and make your comparison. Be aware of how much things cost so that as soon as there are any slight increments, you can make adjustments to your shopping list to save where you can. People often aren't aware they are being charged more than they should, and stores rely on this ignorance.

Scouting for Awesome Deals: You should take advantage of discounts whenever they come up. Now, some stores and vendors will claim to offer discounts, but what they really do is keep the price the same and show you a marked-up price as the former price. If you've been doing a good job of tracking prices, you'll know when they're being shady (and hopefully stop shopping with businesses like this). When there's a legitimate discount, use it, but remember to use it only for your needs. An outfit or a game console could be 50% off, but is it a need? That's a good question to ask before you rush to buy it. Deals could also be in the form of rebates or coupons, which can help you save more than you realize. There's a study that demonstrated that using coupons could save you and your family 6.4% of your money when buying clothing, food, and household items, as well as spending on entertainment and other miscellaneous things. You could also consider buying used items to save yourself money.

Following a Budget: This is the cornerstone of remaining frugal. You'll spend smarter and save more by budgeting specific amounts of money to different parts of your life. Having to sit down to draw up a budget is not an appealing thought; however, it's something you'll be thankful you made yourself do it. Budgeting will help you see where your money goes and show you chances where you can trim the fat, so to speak, on your spending. The best budgets allow you to be flexible. Be careful of getting so rigid with it that you don't have fun or cannot use the other frugality principles.

Using Credit to Your Credit: Credit cards can be a menace, but only if you don't have the right mindset about how to make them work for you. It's supposed to be used like a debit card, in the sense that you only ever make purchases when you have the funds for them in your bank account. In addition, you'll find some credit cards give you rewards with each use. Beware, though, you may be tempted to spend more than usual with a credit card, so budget for it. However, if you don't think you can handle having a credit card, then the next best thing to do is stop using them and destroy the ones you have. This way, you're only spending the money you have.

Making the Most of Your Resources: You may not realize it, but sometimes you don't have to dip into your money. You'll learn this truth if you've decided to try frugality on for size. Some things absolutely should be bought or invested in, and others aren't worth a cent. What are these things? The truth is it depends on you and your experience. It depends on where you are in life. What will help you determine what's worth your money is asking yourself what you could repurpose or reuse instead of buying. For instance, why spend money on new kitchen napkins when you could recycle old, worn-out clothes instead? Why get a new trash can for your car when empty tissue boxes could serve the same purpose? Why throw out glass and plastic containers when you can use them to hold other items? Why get new furniture when you can reupholster it to look as good as new? These are just a few ways you can stretch out your resources.

Handling Things Yourself: There's nothing you can't learn to do on the internet. There's always a tool or instructional video to help you work out how to fix or install things yourself, which is great because you'll gain new skills that could become marketable while saving you money. This doesn't mean you should do it all yourself. Some things may be way above your head, so it's best to hire a pro — especially with plumbing, electricity, etc.

The Historical Evolution of Frugality

Frugality has always been a thing. If you travel through time and space to ancient Rome, you'll find the people considered being frugal, something to be proud of. It was common sense and part and parcel of their way of life. During the epoch of Stoicism, it made sense that people were frugal because the idea of being Stoic involves restraining yourself rather than allowing your impulses to control you. The ancient Romans knew it was best to be practical and sensible with their resources, not just for their individual lives but for society as a whole. The same can be said of the Medieval days, especially when people had to deal with scarcity. Frugality wasn't merely a philosophy but a necessity because without it, many would have died. People learned the value of trade by bartering, getting involved in agriculture, and cooperating with one another to satisfy their needs.

Analyze the Industrial Revolution, and you'll find more than ever, frugality became more relevant. The industrialization of civilization meant people were carried away by their desire to consume. So, frugality helped to ensure people managed their money and other resources in a way that wouldn't lead to waste until the onset of rampant consumerism in recent years. In these present times, frugality is making a comeback because life has never been as uncertain as it appears today. You don't even need to turn on the news to witness this. Every other month, everyday household items go up in price more than enough for anyone to notice. Threats of war, fresh outbreaks of disease, and other things mean it is necessary to become wise about one's spending habits. So, you're doing the right thing by educating yourself about how to keep your money, to patch the holes through which your priceless pennies could drop and leave you broke and insecure.

Chapter 2

The Psychology of Spending

Part of becoming a frugal person is learning about the psyche of spending. Often, people make their financial decisions based on emotions. But what exactly are the drivers that cause people to use their dollars the way they do?

The Psyche of Spending

Hedonistic Tendencies: Humans are naturally interested in anything that makes them feel pleasure. Often, that means not thinking about the long-term implications of their choices. When you're a bit of a hedonist, you tend to spend only for the thrill of it, spontaneously splurging on a pricey meal, a weekend at a luxurious hotel, a gadget you don't need but want, because it would make you feel good to have these things. You do it for the dopamine hit you get from swiping your cards and taking home your brand-new "toys."

Social Position: Depending on your culture, you may have been raised to believe that spending is how you demonstrate you're truly successful and have made your mark in life. If you don't spend, you're looked down upon, sometimes to the point of being ostracized. Because of this, many channel their money toward obtaining luxury items, choosing to live in locations that are considered "exclusive," and making a point of visiting the hottest, most elite vacation spots — all in a bid to signal to society, "Look at me! I've made it in life!"

Crafting Identity: Spending can also be influenced by your desire to be seen in a certain light. So, you spend money on clothes and other things that make you look like the sort of person you think receives respect and deference. You also spend money on any hobbies that you believe make you who you are.

Dealing with Difficult Emotions: Some people spend because they're out of their depth emotionally. They haven't developed healthy coping mechanisms for overwhelming feelings, and they escape by spending money. This practice is called "retail therapy," but it's not exactly therapy if it only plunges you into a financial hole by the end of the day.

Biases That Drive Spending in This Consumerist Culture

Several biases affect your spending choices. Here's a look at the most common ones.

Loss Aversion Bias: The *loss aversion* bias is when you're worried that if you don't spend money, you'll miss out on a deal or a rare experience. The human brain is wired to avoid loss as much as possible, so you spend money on things have no need for. You funnel your money into things that don't belong on your budget because you don't want to lose.

Present Bias: Another thing humans are naturally wired to do is consider the here and now above the future. What does this imply? You want to gratify all your desires right away, even if it would serve you better to wait a little longer. So, on a whim, you buy things at the cost of your future security, eschewing the need to save or ensure you can retire with ease.

Confirmation Bias: When this bias is in action, it causes you to ignore every bit of information that doesn't line up with your present beliefs, no matter how real and present they are. In other words, you don't want to consider for a moment that your spending choices may be wrong for you and that there may be a better, more sustainable way to handle your money than you're presently doing.

Social Proof: Humans want to do as others around them do, to fit in and enjoy a sense of belonging. So, you may emulate others in the way they spend, not realizing that they may earn more than you do and therefore can sustain their choices, while for you, it would be a struggle.

These are just a few of many biases that could drive you to make choices that don't serve your future self.

Your Individual Traits and Spending Choices

You may have the sort of personality that leads you to spend more than others. For instance, if you have a neurodiverse condition like ADHD, you may be more impulsive with your spending because you need to feel some emotion. You need the dopamine release new "toys" bring and are more likely to shell out more dollars than you should. On the flip side, if you're the sort of person who doesn't struggle with impulsivity and you've mastered self-control, then it follows that you will pause before splurging and probably decide against it. This isn't to say there's any shame in impulsivity; whether it's from a condition or upbringing, there's still hope for you to get things under control.

Other factors that influence your spending choices include the things that you value the most, as well as your childhood experiences. If you grew up in a culture that values spending, then it makes sense that you'd do the same. Being frugal might come easily to you if you live in a frugal household. On the flip side, it could also be that your parents or guardians were so frugal that you grew up and did a 180, refusing to live that way.

Finally, there's the matter of whether or not you're financially literate. If you are, you know about handling your debt, investing your money so it works for you, and setting a budget to keep yourself from going overboard with spending. If you aren't financially literate, it's only natural to make financial decisions that make you shake your head at yourself in hindsight.

The danger of not checking your habits is very real. How many times have you been one paycheck away from being in deep trouble? How deep a hole have you dug yourself into debt? How often have you chanted the mantra "Treat yourself!" only to wind up feeling buyer's remorse once the dopamine has worn off? The pitfalls of not being careful include falling into the trap set by marketers and advertisers, losing money on impulse buys, feeling anxious about falling behind on payments, and destroying any chances of attaining true financial stability. So, good on you for taking the time to educate yourself.

Practical Tools to Control Your Spending Impulses

1. **Begin Tracking Where Every Cent Goes**. How much goes to food, rent, clothing, bills, entertainment, and savings? By using apps designed for this purpose, it will be easy to know where your money goes and how to control your spending better.
2. **Always Question Every Spending Urge You Get**. If you need to stand for 20 seconds before an item to realize you don't need it, do that. By creating this buffer of time between picking an item and putting it in your cart, you're far more likely to put down what you don't want.
3. **Create Subaccounts for Each Section of Your Budget and Only Spend from the Relevant Account, Depending on What You're Getting**. This way, if you're out of money for a habit like sports betting, you know you cannot dip into

any of your other accounts once you've spent it all.

4. **Clear Your Email of All Marketing Attempts**. Send all advertising and marketing messages straight to spam after unsubscribing. You'll be surprised to find you're no longer spending on those services, which may have been useless in the first place.
5. **Unsubscribe from Services You Don't Need**. Do you really need to be on Netflix, Hulu, *and* Disney+? Is there a chapter option that has *all* the shows you seek that you could switch to? Look that up and change.
6. **Always Pay Yourself First.** Whenever money comes in, the first thing you should do is set aside a specific portion to pay yourself. You can use an automatic debit function to help you with this, so you don't have the chance to second guess yourself.
7. **Are There Credit Cards You Have But Don't Need?** Consider putting them on a temporary freeze, and with time, don't be surprised to find that you've completely forgotten about them. The beauty of keeping your cards "icy" is that

you won't be able to spend willy-nilly like you used to. Your impulse will automatically be blocked.

8. **Consider Going Shopping with Cash Only**. This is genius because if you don't have the money on you, you already know you can't overspend. Sure, you could use your app, but not having cash forces you to pause and reconsider whether that impulse buy is necessary or not.
9. **Have Set Days in the Week When You Do Not Spend, No Matter What.** This will force you to notice more and more what you do with your money, pay attention to what triggers you to want to spend, and help you learn to say no.
10. **Fall in Love with the Idea of Being a Minimalist**. Choose to have few possessions rather than a lot.

Chapter 3

Building a Frugal Mindset

The way to be frugal is to understand how a frugal person thinks. But what exactly makes up a frugal mindset in the first place? Many people think it's about pinching your pennies so hard that you don't spend anything and you don't get to live your life. Some think it's being such a scrooge that you'd rather mooch off of others than use your own money. But really, what it's about is deciding your long-term goals and comfort are far more important than whatever your interest is at the moment.

The Components of a Frugal Mindset

Recognizing That Value Supersedes Price: Your frugal self is unfazed by price if it means you'll get a good bang for your buck. With this attitude, you want items that will last long and give you little to no need to fix them over and over again. You spend money on clothes that will not wear out in a matter of weeks or months. You know it's much better, healthier, and cheaper to enjoy meals at home than to spend money on pricey restaurant meals, which probably taste nothing like what you could whip up at home. It's finding new ways to entertain yourself that don't require paying for a subscription service or anything of the sort.

Understanding Needs Matter More Than Wants: The things you want are things you could live without. The things you need, however, are non-negotiable. How can you tell the wants apart from needs? Your wants pop up impulsively in your mind. They are only fleeting and nothing serious or lasting. Do you have to get a brand new shirt simply because there's a stain you can't get rid of on an old one, or would it be better to bleach or dye it? Is a newer, larger television going to help you see things that you couldn't before on your favorite TV show? Of course not. However, you need food, water, and a place to lay your head. You need a means to move about from place to place. These are essentials.

Choosing to Delay Gratification: The world is set up to make people less patient than ever in the history of humankind. If you want frozen food to thaw out, why wait hours when you can pop it in the microwave and have it ready in twenty minutes or less? If you want to order something, why wait a week when it can get to you overnight? Well, if you apply this instant gratification mindset to your finances, you'll see how quickly you can run into a lot of trouble. Being frugal means being at peace with waiting, disciplining yourself to wait until the time is right before spending on things you want.

Creative Resourcefulness: Make your own lemonade rather than go to the store. You're about recycling, upcycling, looking for deals, and using the more affordable versions of things.

Strategies for Developing a Positive Relationship with Money

You need to develop a better relationship with money if you plan to keep it. So, here are some strategies to help you with the process.

Recognize Money Is a Tool: You have to understand what money is. It's meant to help you secure your freedom. Money isn't freedom itself. Once you grasp that, you'll be more than happy to keep your money rather than spend it because it gives you the means to do whatever you like. You can take up a new hobby, go to school to learn something new, help the people in your life, or whatever else you desire.

Shift Your Mindset from Stockpiling Material Goods to Gaining Enriching Experience: When you value experiences that make your heart sing with joy and bliss, you will be determined to restrain your spending. You want a life that feels fulfilling, and you'll have discovered that no amount of new things will be enough to make and keep you happy.

Get Educated on What Money Is: Have you always winged it? Well, you need to stop. It's time to be strategic about your financial choices, and that means you should study everything you can about money. Learn about personal finance, investment, and making your money work for you. The more you learn, the more respect you'll have for the dollars in your hands, and the more likely it is you'll reserve them for better things rather than wasting them on more and more needless stuff.

Consider Your Choices First, Then Commit Afterward: For instance, assume you currently owe money. If you choose to save up some money before you handle your debt, you have to carefully think about why before settling on that course of action. After some consideration, you may have realized that each time you pay off your debt when due, you're left with too little to take care of yourself and the other essentials.

In the same way, if you'd rather invest money than save or vice versa, think about why and ask yourself if that option lines up with your financial goals.

Make Saving a Game and Become Extremely Competitive at It. Who are you competing against? Yourself. Work out how much money you need to spend on essentials every month, and then you can save what's left. Always be on the lookout for opportunities to spend less so you can see how much more you save each month or week. Saving is essential not only for emergencies but to give you the feeling of being financially stable and secure. With this state of mind, it'll be easier for you to recognize the opportunities to make more money that you may have overlooked because you were too anxious and focused on the one income stream you had.

Be Grateful and Satisfied with Your Life: Frugal people learn to look at what they have and realize it's a lot to be thankful for. As a result, they aren't moved by ads or marketing material. They don't care about having the latest iPhone and recognize it's not even worth the price. They don't care about needing to look as trendy as the next person, nor are they interested in splurging on designer items. By choosing to appreciate what you have, you kill the urge to splurge senselessly.

Exercises to Shift to a Frugal Mindset

Work with a 24-Hour Rule. Before you make any spending decision, wait for at least 24 hours. If the impulse to buy this thing is still powerful at the end of this time, and you cannot find a justifiable reason not to have it, then wait another 24 hours. This gives you more than enough time to clear your mind. You may find you don't actually need this impulse buy.

Follow the One-in, One-Out Rule. In other words, you need to be proactive about decluttering your space. You don't want to become one of those people who hoard items to the point where they don't even remember what they have. Why? Because you may find yourself spending money on what you already have, which is wasteful. So whenever you get something new, look for something old to get rid of. Another advantage of this is if you truly value the things you possess, you'll be more reluctant to spend money on something new because it means getting rid of something old and treasured.

Start up a Weekly Journal Where You Write Down Everything You're Grateful For. Every day, take about 5 to 10 minutes to write down what it is about your life that you appreciate. By practicing gratitude this way, you become aware of how little you need. You realize that you actually have an abundant life, and it is this understanding that keeps you from making impulsive financial decisions.

Make a List of the Things You Want Versus the Things You Need. Every time a new thing pops up in your mind, categorize it and put it in the proper place on your list. When you realize something is only a want, think about alternative ways you can get it without having to spend a dime or at least too much money.

Value Functionality Over Style. It doesn't matter whether it's your clothes or how you travel. If you take economy or first class, guess what? You're still heading to the same destination, aren't you? If you book the priciest room in a hotel, or you book a reasonably priced one, you're still going to sleep, aren't you? So, you have to develop the proper perspective when it comes to spending.

Detach from Brand Names and Focus on Function: Just because a device is not an iPhone doesn't mean that it is not practical. In fact, more often than not, it is more reasonable to have any other kind of device besides the iPhone. Fun fact: iPhone fanatics are great examples of people who allow their sentiments and emotions to control their spending decisions. When you objectively compare the iPhone to an Android device, for instance, you'll find the latter has more functionality than the former, and the prices are more reasonable, too. This behavior is also typical of people who insist on using Samsung rather than any other Android product. Detach yourself from the implied value of brand names and focus on true value when you're making your purchases.

Be Efficient When It Comes to Using Energy. LEDs are much better than incandescent bulbs, so consider making the switch. If you're the kind of person who leaves home with every electronic device still plugged in and turned on, you need to cut that out now because you're losing money by wasting power. These things may seem insignificant, but you'll be surprised to find how much money you can save by simply taking time to turn things off before you head out the door. If you do this for a month, you'll be impressed with how much your utility bills have dropped.

Avoid Spending Money on Single-Use Plastics. Not only are these terrible for the environment, but you can't use them for anything else, so what's the point? It's better to choose reusable bottles, bags, containers, etc. Whenever possible, choose products that can be refilled rather than items you can only use once and throw out.

Stop Wasting Food. So what if you're unable to finish your meal? Does that mean you should hook it into the trash? Of course not. You can always store it in the fridge and then use it the next day to make a different meal or warm it up and eat it as it is. Food is primarily meant to give you the energy to move around and do things, so it doesn't always have to taste as if it just came off of a five-star chef's cooking stove. This doesn't mean you do not deserve to eat well; it only means that you shouldn't waste food. Get creative and think about how you can turn last night's leftovers into a brand-new dish, and you'll never have to worry about not enjoying your meals.

Do Your Shopping Locally. Having to transport food from one country to another costs money. One way or another, you pay for that cost, even if you can't see the breakdown on your receipt. Well, if you haven't done this already, take a walk around your local neighborhood and see what's being sold around you. Not only is it the kind and neighborly thing to do to support local businesses, but you'll also find you get much better deals as a result. You can check out second-hand shops for clothing and other items, farmers' markets for food items, and craft fares for materials you can use in your DIY projects.

Take Pride in Choosing Not to Upgrade. Now, this isn't meant to imply that you shouldn't spoil yourself every now and then. However, you should be on top of the desire to swap out what you have for what is "better." In other words, if what you have already works, what's the point in replacing it just because there's a new model? Do you really have to get the next model of your phone if your current one is working just fine? Do you really need to keep up with the latest fashion trends, or can you simply create your own style with what you already have? If something stops working in your house, do you need to get a brand new one, or can you fix it? If there's something you want, is it possible you could borrow from someone else instead of buying another new item if you don't use it all the time? Beware of the natural tendency of humans to be attracted to new and flashy things. Remember, if it does the same job as something you already have, then it's not really new. It's a pointless purchase.

Chapter 4

Budgeting and Financial Planning

The foundation of financial security is budgeting. If you want the finances you've always dreamed of, you can't get around budgeting. You need to have a plan in place for how each of your dollars will be spent. Think of every dollar as a soldier and your life as a war. If you only ever send your soldiers out to specific points of the battle, you may find yourself getting ambushed by enemies from other directions. You have to strategically assign each dollar a specific task. The way to do this is to create a budget. There's no one-size-fits-all budget that you can plug your finances into and use. This is because everyone's different when it comes to how much money they earn, as well as what their financial goals are for the short, medium, and long term.

Why Should You Budget?

For starters, when you have a budget in place, you have clarity on how to achieve the goals you've set for yourself financially. When it's clear what you intend to accomplish for your financial well-being, it becomes easier to control your impulse to spend. You automatically place yourself in a position of power, and every decision you make is geared towards your financial success. It's the difference between diffused light and focusing that light on a single spot using a magnifying glass. A budget gives you focus, and that focus ensures that as you continue to follow the plan, you will accomplish what you want.

Having a budget in place also means you'll be able to handle your debts better. Some people allow their debts to pile up for months and even years because they have no idea how to approach them. Why? They don't have a budget, which would also contain a structured plan for how to pay off debts. Are you currently struggling with a few unpaid debts? Take the time to craft a budget, and you'll be amazed to find that clearing your debts shouldn't have been as hard as it was for you this whole time. Budgets are excellent for managing debts because you are forced to prioritize what you need over what you want, and you can channel the money you would have spent on your wants toward settling your debts. Eventually, you'll be done paying them. Then, guess what? You begin saving the money that you used to put toward debt instead, which means more financial security for you.

Living a life without a budget means you may not be prepared for emergencies that come your way. What happens if you need to repair your car because it broke down all of a sudden? What if there's a friend who needs help? With a budget, you can set aside funds for these miscellaneous and unforeseen circumstances. You'll be able to sleep better because you know no matter what comes your way, you can handle it without taking too much of a hit financially. If you're living your life without a budget, it's like walking a tightrope at the highest altitude with nothing underneath you to catch you. Your budget is your safety net, so you know, even if you fall off of that tightrope, you're not going to splatter like a bug on a windshield when you approach the ground.

What are the reasons compelling enough for you to have a budget? Well, would you like to have a home of your own someday or go for a dream vacation? Would you like to help your parents finally retire so they can enjoy life? Whatever your goals are, having a budget makes it more likely that you'll accomplish them. You'll assign your dollars exactly where they need to go. You'll immediately catch any holes that are a drain on your resources and plug them up right away, thanks to your budget.

Consider crafting a budget if you haven't at this point. There's nothing quite like the feeling of knowing that there's money in your bank account. It is so liberating to know that even if you lost every stream of income right now, you'd still have enough money to keep yourself going for at least six months to a year. Are you nowhere near this point? Don't worry about it. You can begin today. Once you start with your budget, it will only take a little time before you finally attain that level of financial security and even surpass that.

Creating a Personalized, Realistic Budget

As mentioned before, you can't take another person's budget and apply it to your situation. Here's how to build your own.

Begin By Keeping Track of Your Income. Whether you only have one job or several, put it all together. Figure out how much you have coming in from all your side hustles, investments, and salaries every month or week.

Group Your Expenses into Different Categories. Certain costs, like your subscriptions, rent, and utilities, are fixed and will recur. Other costs are variable, like your groceries. Think about everything you spend money on and put them in their proper category.

Clearly Distinguish between the Needs and Wants in Your Expenses. When you've done this, you need to first channel money towards the needs because those are the more essential things.

Choose a Budgeting Method That Works for You and Tweak It as Needed. Here are some methods to get you started:

1. **The 50/30/20 Budget:** Fifty percent of your income should go towards your needs, 30% towards your wants, and 20% towards repaying your debt, saving, and making investments that pay off later.
2. **The Zero-Based Budget:** The focus of this style of budgeting is that when you're done, there shouldn't be a single dollar unaccounted for or left over. If you notice at the end of the month that you still have some money left over, that means you need to adjust your budget until you achieve a flat zero every time.
3. **Envelope Budgeting:** The style of budgeting originally was done using envelopes. The idea

is to allocate specific amounts of money to separate accounts or envelopes. Each digital envelope is meant to handle a specific thing. For instance, you could have a digital envelope for your online subscriptions, another for dining out, another for rent, etc. Whenever an envelope is empty, you can't spend money from any other envelope because each envelope is specifically allocated to an expense.

Tracking and Managing Your Expenses for Long-Term Goals

Having a budget doesn't mean you shouldn't live your life. It does mean you need to keep track of where your money is going if you hope to be successful financially and attain any other goals that you may have in mind. With that said, you can use the following tracking techniques.

Select a Digital Platform to Help You Stay on Top of Where Every Dollar Goes. Excellent apps you can use for this, such as YNAB, Mint, etc. There are also banking apps that have integrated budget-tracking services. They can show you how you spend your money.

Pay Attention to the Small Expenses. You may think that they don't matter much, but they do. It doesn't matter if it's a loaf of bread or a cup of coffee. Note every expense down. Even if whatever you bought only costs a few cents, it should be tracked in your financial journal.

Link Every Credit and Debit Card and Bank Account to a Specific Platform for More Accurate Tracking. This way, you don't have to hop around too much to figure out your finances.

Review Your Income and Expenditure Every Month. Otherwise, there's no point in tracking. The information you notice will help you make needed adjustments to your budget and get a better hold of your spending.

Chapter 5

Overcoming Frugality Challenges

Becoming frugal and watching your spending isn't a walk in the park. There are societal challenges and pressures you have to face when you choose to live this way. If you plan to have any success, you must be prepared for the obstacles that will be on your path and know how to triumph over each one.

Challenges to Frugality

The Fear of Missing Out (FOMO): Thanks to social media, people are afraid of missing out. No one remembers that it is impossible for you to be a part of everything, everywhere, all at once. Yet that doesn't stop them from succumbing to the pressure to try. As you scroll through social media, you find that your perfectly curated feed places a lot of pressure on you to buy this, that, or the other. People are actively engaged in the business of presenting you with fake lifestyles to sell you luxury brands, and more often than not, people fall for this.

Look at the recent Stanley Cup debacle, for instance. People were tripping over one another to get the pink or red Stanley Cups. Never mind that these cups were made by a company that partnered with another actively supporting genocide, as at the time of writing. Society pressures you into wanting possessions and experiences that are not necessary. You're convinced that you want this bauble and that if you think about it, you aren't really even interested in it. That's the power of advertising and marketing. It's meant to make you feel like you're missing out on something if you don't click the Add to Cart button now and buy it.

Feelings of Guilt. Pay attention to the way people address or talk about frugality, and you are immediately hit with the assumption that you aren't a fun person. You don't enjoy life. You're depriving yourself for nothing. If you listen to these people long enough, you'll start to feel guilty about not letting yourself "enjoy" your income. Listen a little longer, and next thing you know, you're making purchases that don't make sense. Humans are naturally wired to be afraid of losing things or losing out. So, if you internalize the messages about frugality being a terrible thing, it's natural for you to head in the opposite direction.

Viewing Yourself as Being Cheap. Another problem with society's perception of frugality is the assumption that you're cheap. If this is the same misconception you have of this way of life, naturally, you'll be averse to it. The people who love you may have the best intentions for you, and yet they won't understand that you have chosen to be this way, not because you're suffering but because you care about your well-being. They may guilt trip you into making huge spends that you didn't plan for. You may give in, too, because you don't want them to judge you as a terrible person or ostracize you for not wanting to spend when you are way over your budget.

You May Feel Terribly Alone on Your Frugal Journey. It's not easy to find people who see life the same way you do when it comes to finances. It appears many people have that "YOLO" mentality, assuming that you only live once, and therefore, you should live responsibly. When your dad just bought another sports car, your mom just bought another house, and your friends are buying things left, right, and center, it's kind of hard not to give in to the pressure to be like these people. You look like the odd person out, the party pooper who appears to be setting themselves up as better than others because you refuse to spend. You feel misunderstood and all on your own for choosing to be frugal.

So now that you understand the most common challenges that you have to contend with as you become a frugal person, the question is, how do you overcome these challenges?

1. Get in touch with your values. These are the things that matter to you the most. If you know what your values are, it is hard for other people to dissuade you from them or make you feel bad for doing what you must to stick with them.
2. Rather than look at frugality or something you're doing in the meantime, look at it as your way of life. Accept that you are now a frugal person. That's just the way you do things.
3. What is it about certain social media accounts that appear to trigger your spending urge? You should unfollow and block them immediately so you don't have to deal with that temptation anymore. As an added bonus, when you block and unfollow these accounts, the algorithm will learn not to show you content like that with time.

4. Take your power back by reframing what frugality means to you. Think of it as something empowering. Rather than assume that it is stealing your freedom and ability to enjoy life, instead understand that being frugal allows you to become intentional with your resources. See your frugal decisions as a way to set yourself free from the bondage of senseless spending.
5. Find balance in your frugal lifestyle by allowing yourself joy in something now and then. You could spend money on a special experience or a treat that you really love.
6. Remind yourself why you decided that you'd like to be frugal in the first place. When you remember your long-term goals and how amazing you'll feel when you accomplish them, it's easier for you to be at peace with your choices, regardless of what the peanut gallery says about them.
7. Indicate clearly and openly with the people in your life about your choices. If they truly love you, they will respect your decision to be frugal. If they continue to cross your boundaries, then you probably should consider minimizing your

contact with these people or parting ways with them.

8. Find a community of like-minded people who understand the power of being frugal. If you can't find them in person, you can definitely find them in online forums. Being a part of a community is a helpful thing because they'll offer you advice and help you see new, interesting ways to save money that you may be unaware of.
9. Keep a financial journal, and every time you make an impulse buy that you feel buyer's remorse about, write about what triggered you to make the purchase in the first place. By keeping track of your triggers, you'll eventually notice a pattern, and you'll know what to do to get ahead of them so you don't succumb to them in the future.
10. Every time you come across advertising or marketing material, listen or read mindfully. Pay attention to the words being used and notice any feelings that arise in you as a result of reading or hearing them. With time, it will be difficult to ignore the fact that every other marketing and

advertising piece is screaming at you to buy. You'll see it all for the manipulation that it is, and you'll find it easier to say no thanks.

Chapter 6

Sustaining Financial Security through Frugality

When you think of financial freedom, what comes to mind? Surely, it's a lot more than having a fat bank account, isn't it? Being financially free means finally breaking up with the anxiety that bothers you every day when you look at your bank account balance and wonder if it'll be enough to sustain you until your next paycheck. It's knowing you're set for life and that when excellent opportunities for investing and growing your money come your way, you'll be able to take advantage of them. This is what it means to have financial security. Why should you want this for yourself?

Reasons to Become Financially Secure

For starters, you'll always have freedom of choice. When you first begin your frugal journey, you'll have to forsake certain things for cheaper alternatives. However, when you finally accomplish your goal of financial security and freedom, a whole world of options opens up to you. You no longer have to pick something based on how much money you have. Because you can afford to go for what you prefer, in other words, financial security means that you choose to do, be, and have things that you want, and not because you must.

Another aspect of financial security that most people don't think about is the fact that you finally have location liberty. It doesn't make sense if you have all the money in the world and yet don't have the ability to move from place to place. True financial freedom means you can pick up and move from one place to the next without worrying about whether you can afford it or not.

Attaining financial security is a necessary life goal to have because once you achieve it, you can be the person you've always wanted to be. You're no longer confined to what your pockets or bank accounts dictate you can or can't do. If you're the sort of person who's always valued spending time with the people you love, you can do that at last. You no longer have to live each day tethered to your laptop, answering to a boss. You can focus on the things that matter to you in life, like your special hobbies or personal development. You never again have to live your life around someone else's expectations and obligations for you.

When the storms of life hit you, you are prepared to handle them. They could be major storms or regular storms, but it wouldn't matter to you because you know you have the financial means to take care of yourself. Is the economy poor? No problem. You're doing just fine. Is there a sudden bill that you have to handle? No problem. You've got enough money saved up, and your dollars are working to bring in more dollars. You no longer have to incur unnecessary debt. A truly financially secure person can focus on building generational wealth and leaving behind a legacy for the people they love. You also have the means to invest in causes that are near and dear to your heart.

Financial security is the gift that keeps on giving. Why? Imagine living a life where you no longer have to say yes to things that you don't care about. You stop saying yes only because you're trying to make a paycheck to keep your life together. You no longer operate from a financially desperate position. Since you only do what you're passionate about, it means you give the best of yourself to the world, and that's a wonderful thing.

Take a look at the world around you, and you'll find many people are struggling with anxiety, depression, and stress. If you do a bit of digging, you'll find that a huge reason for this mental distress is financial. Can you imagine what it'll feel like when you finally achieve financial security? Imagine setting yourself free from the shackles of mental distress. Imagine waking up when you want to versus when an alarm clock pulls you out of bed before you're ready. Picture a version of yourself who eats, sleeps, and rests well because you can afford to. This could be you if you put in the work and start being frugal today.

Investing with a Frugal Mindset

It's awesome that you've decided to live a frugal life, but why not take it a step further? Have you considered investing? You definitely should. What is investing about anyway? It's about taking the money you have and allowing it to grow. You can put your money in stocks, bonds, and other financial assets that are likely to keep going up in value. Choosing to be frugal means you'll have more than enough money left over each week or month to put toward your investments. This means you can attain financial security even faster than you thought possible. You've probably already figured this out, but your budget should have a section specifically dedicated to investments.

There's a symbiotic relationship between frugality and wealth building. You see, the more you can save money by being frugal, the more you'll have to put into different investment vehicles, and the more money you'll pile up in the process. You can invest in the stock market, which is a way to own a portion of companies that are doing well. If you work with a professional financial advisor, they can let you know which of the companies are worth your dollars, and you can plop some money in there and watch your investment rise year after year. If you consider that inflation is always going up, it makes sense to not just work on being frugal and save some money but also invest. That way, regardless of inflation, you are going to be comfortable.

Don't want to invest in the stock market? No problem. You can invest in bonds. This financial investment vehicle requires lending your money to your government or companies and getting it back with interest at a later date. Why might you want to pick bonds over stocks? Because bonds are safer. However, a general rule of thumb in the investment is that the safer the investment vehicle, the slower the growth of your interest or profits. So, it may be worth it to have a balance of stocks and bonds. This way, you know there's something that brings in faster profits, even though it's a bit riskier, and something else that brings in guaranteed profits, even if it takes time.

Another excellent place to park your money is in real estate. When you have enough money to begin buying properties, you should consider doing so because, generally, property values should go up. Even if all you can afford are fixer-uppers, you can fix them up and sell them for a higher value than you originally got them. Combining investing with frugal living is a great way to supercharge your financial security. Whatever you decide, it's important to work with a professional who knows exactly where to invest your money for the best results.

Conclusion

This book has given you everything you need to know to take charge of your financial destiny. There is no reason you should live one more day uncertain about how you're going to fare as you get older. You now have the information you need to make conscious choices about your finances that will serve you in the long run.

Frugal living doesn't have to be hard. As you keep it up, you'll discover there's no better way to live than to be deliberate about where your money goes every day. Each day, you'll be amazed as your savings snowball into something impressive. You'll thank yourself for daring to walk this not-so-easy path that pays off in the end. You know how the saying goes. You could choose to live life in easy mode now and hard later, or hard now and easy later. The wonderful thing about frugal living is that you'll discover it's not so hard once you have the proper mindset. By the time you achieve financial security, whatever that means to you, you'll be glad that you started.

The ultimate goal here is not to stockpile dollars just for the sake of having them or for bragging rights. It's about the feeling of fulfillment that you receive after having accomplished your financial goals. It's about being in an empowered position where you can bless others and help them accomplish the same thing that you have. It is setting yourself free from the double-headed monster of capitalism and consumerism to discover that bliss and joy are intrinsic values that cannot be found in anything outside of yourself.

You may believe in the law of attraction and the power of positivity. However, you need action to back up those things. If you want to experience true abundance, you have to be willing to put in the work. Interestingly enough, the more you learn to pay yourself first and set some money aside, the more money-making opportunities will come your way. If you want to put that to the test, there's only one thing to do. Put everything you've learned in this book into practice and see for yourself. Someday soon, you'll find yourself in such a beautiful financial space that you'll be glad you gave frugal living a shot.

References

Denton, J. (2021). Frugal Living: How to Manage Your Money, Set up a Budget & Achieve Financial Success (Learn the Fundaments of Personal Finance). James Denton.

Farrell, C. (2011). The New Frugality: How to Consume Less, Save More, and Live Better. Bloomsbury Press.

Faunillan, F., & Davidson, J. (2015). Frugal Living - When Less Means More. Mendon Cottage Books.

Johnson, H. D. (2023, November 30). What Does Frugal Mean? Bankrate. https://www.bankrate.com/banking/what-does-frugal-mean/

Jordan, T. (2023, April 11). This is the REAL Meaning of Being Frugal (Hint: It's Not Depriving Yourself). Atypical Finance. https://www.atypicalfinance.com/determining-what-you-value-how-to-become-frugal/

Leung, A. (2023, September 7). Cheap vs. Frugal. Medium. https://medium.com/@andrewleung14/cheap-vs-frugal-d6e22747dd82

Radjou, N., Prabhu, J., & The Economist. (2015). Frugal Innovation: How to Do More with Less. PublicAffairs.

Robin, V., Dominguez, J. R., & Tilford, M. (2008). Your Money or Your Life: 9 Steps to Transforming Your Relationship with Money and Achieving Financial Independence. Penguin Books.

Sheehy, K., & Bundrick, H. M. (2022, June 9). Frugal Living Guide: 35 Ways to Find Serious Savings. NerdWallet. https://www.nerdwallet.com/article/finance/frugal-living-guide

Printed by BoD™in Norderstedt, Germany

9 780648 646976